Laugh louder

Poems by Gaza

1) Building of sin	28) First disco
2) Rotten luck	29) Beautiful fool
3) Sweet Geisha	30) Only ugly should marry
4) Jenny Penny	31) Robot love
5) Schmocking	32) Coping with change
6) Blind drunk	33) Cross pollination
7) Whoa !	34) Life's rules
8) The Captain is dead	35) Out of it
9) JD tripping	36) Trantastic
10) First time nearly	37) Dog's life
11) Jaded	38) Count down
12) Alien Fred	39) Scarlet arachnid
13) Crocodile's shoes	40) True love
14) In my mind	41) Butt of the joke
15) Hoppy rabbit	42) Private time
16) Mary had a little duck	43) The best sex
17) My love poem	44) Horse racing
18) Love ship	45) Another love poem
19) Beach farce	46) Hey fiddle fiddle
20) Don't tell the kids	47) Coming out
21) Light me up	48) Rain dance
22) Bo Bo and Jo Jo	49) Food of love
23) Dr Strangelove	50) Ogre
24) Nothing	51) I don't but I do
25) Dodgy Ruby	52) Fly
26) Party in my head	53) Cider goggles
27) Hazy haze	54) Happy rising

Building Of Sin

1)

I've created a
building of sin ,
you can do what
you like within .
The bedrooms are
the best rooms by far
as they all contain
their own bar .
The ladies are
easily led ;
but alas it's
all in my head

Rotten Luck

2)

A fly flew into my cider
followed by a hungry spider,
they both became ever so drunk
then they were eaten by a skunk

3)

Sweet Geisha

Sweet sexy geisha my
dreams bring me to you ,
but in reality ; her
indoors 'll do :o]

4)

Jenny Penny

Humpty Dumpty Stylee

Jenny Penny stood
on a wall,
Jenny Penny 10
feet tall.
All the Kings
forces
and my
uncle Ben,
came to
look up
Jennies skirt
once again
Ever the Gentleman I
averted my eyes of course.

Shmoking. :o]

5)

Welcome to my
magical, mystical world ;
where all life's' myths
and secrets can be unfurled.
I've dissected a demon
to see inside ,
I found out that is
where the black fairies hide .
It is said that the fairies
come out at night ,
and would give even
the most hardened a fright.
When I was drunk once
they came to visit me ,
but let me be after I
Shared the JD

Blind Drunk

6)

I live inside my eyes
and see no further
than my nose ,
and that is why I
fell over and broke
my fucking toes

Whoa !

7}

On my knees in the garden,
saying my prayers and
asking the odd why ......?
I look up for answers
and see Gods' bollocks
swinging across the sky :o]

The Captain Is Dead

8)

No dawn horn this morning
just a dawn flop ,
I must admit it caught
me on the hop .
Early to rise is all
I remember ,
I don't know of a
dawn flaccid member .
It worked so well when
I gave it a toss
yet in the morn'
it was all at a loss :o]

9)
J.d Tripping

I trip and fall down stairs
in true style farce ,
I land upside down
looking up my arse :o]

10)
First Time, Nearly :o}

She took down her pants ,
I said what's that fucking smell ?
My first thought ; if I touch
that I'm going to hell .
She moves closer , boobs swinging
fierce down by her knees ;
my next thought is get me the
fuck out of here please :o}

11)
Jaded

There are crazy
funny people
running through
my mind unaided .
I love their fun
and antics although
they leave me
kind of jaded

Alien Fred

12)

A little red spaceship brought
alien Fred down from space .
His greeting was to sit on my
head and fart in my face .
And of course I deemed this
to be awfully rude ,
but what he done with
the cucumber I found crude .
He pulled this cucumber from
his arse and gave me it to lick ,
yet as he drew nearer to me
it made me feel ever so sick .
I didn't want to be rude
but that cucumber was rank ;
in fact I'll go much further than that ,
the fucking thing stank .
Nevertheless I felt obliged to
give it a gentle lick ,
but what I didn't realise was ;
it was his fucking dick   :o]

Crocodile's Shoes

13)

My new shoes are
kind of snappy
but crocodile
is not happy .
Whilst my shoes
are very neat ,
poor croc' walks around
with bare feet

In My Mind

14)

Searching through the
cupboards in my mind ,
looking out for wholesome
food for thought .
I happen across a
sweet monkey
reading through all
that I have been taught .
The monkey sees me
and spanks himself ,
then puts back my
learning on the shelf .
I then spy my forever
friend Brad ;
he's fixing up his old
land rover .
His karma good , he's
smiling at me ,
there are spanners and
parts all over

Hoppy Rabbit

15)

Hoppy little rabbit
looking all forlorn ,
hoppy little rabbit
crapped over my lawn ,
hoppy little rabbit
is playing ring a ring o' roses ,
hoppy little rabbit
bless it's little myxomatosis

16)
Mary Had A Little Duck (Repost)

Mary had a little duck
she named him tiny Tim ,
born with no legs or wings
he couldn't fly or swim .
Out in the garden one day
where Mary often left Tim ,
he was approached by a big gay swan
who mounted Tim and fucked him :o]

17)
My love poem

I love sexy time
it takes the load
off my sack .

There's no finer sight
than my honey
on her back

Love Ship :o]

18)

Welcome to the love ship
where the dicks are hard
and the pussies pulsating .
Pay no heed if you don't
like the guys or chicks ,
there's always masturbating .
You can kiss, lick, suck
and fuck until you've
had your fill .
But please don't lick
arse if you think
it will make you ill :o]

Beach Farce

19)

We went to the seaside
to celebrate our kid
being top of her class .
She sat down too fast on
her beach ball and her
fanny disappeared up her arse :o]

20)
Don't Tell The Kids :o}

Noddy is an arsehole
postman Pat is a twat ,
for Spongebob and the
Simpsons I will raise my fucking hat :o}

21)
Light Me Up

Turn on your crimson
light and sell me
your wares .
*****

I shall oblige you
with finance if
you invite me upstairs .
****

I want you and need
you to provide me
release .
****

And once I'm done
our contract will
cease

Bo Bo And Jo Jo

22)

Bo bo the hobo
was sucking her dildo
to keep it nice and clean .
*****
Jo Jo the hobo
was licking out Bo bo
the strangest thing I've seen :o}

Dr Strangelove

23)

Sperm worm in hand ,
firm and ready for action ;
Strangelove spies tattoo queen
legs up in traction :o}

Nothing

24)

A crocodile once
said to me ;
nothing he was
eating his dinner you see :o}

25)

Dodgy Ruby

I had a dodgy curry
whilst dining out ,
then the next day I
shit myself inside out .
******

I crapped and crapped until
head and arse went blue ,
shit myself so hard my
ribs went down the loo .
******

So if you're out and you
fancy a curry ,
make sure you can
reach the loo in a hurry :o}

26)

Party In My Head

There's a moth in my ear
smoking cannabis and
it's driving me crazy .
*****

There's a wasp in my eye
taking cocaine and it's
making me so lazy .
*****

The moth made a pass at
the wasp but the wasp stung
him with her cocaine sting .
*****

They sure are having a
party in my head and it's
causing me to sing

Hazy Haze

27)

I see your cocaine smile
beyond the cigarette haze ;
I think I'm smiling through
my cocaine and booze fuelled daze ?
*****
Then hear a grand piano playing
but is it real ?
More than that going on in
my head , I need to heal .
*****
I invite the lady here to
join me for a drink ;
we drink far too much then
put the world to rights I think ?

First Disco :o}

28)

You stare at me for a while
then you ask me to dance ;
making weird shapes with my
arms and legs you've got no chance .
*****
You ask me to kiss you with
nervous smile on your face
but my stomach churns when
you smile and expose your brace .
*****
You put my hand on your breast
you naughty little skank ;
I leave the disco and go home
where I have a wank .
*****
Memories of first disco
frightened life out of me
but I suppose at least it
ended for me in glee :o}

29)

Beautiful Fool

I watch your sexy
pratting about like a tool :
came to the conclusion
you're a beautiful fool

30)

Only Ugly Should Marry :o}

Not a matchmaker per se
yet see mismatches each day
some really do cause dismay .
******
Only ugly should marry
no babies shall they carry
the pretty they must parry .
*****
Pretty on pretty is fun
if ugly turns up get gun
shoot the minger then run .
*****
Run to the pretty safe house
sooth your pretty ears with Strauss
then in milk and champagne douse .
*****
No guilt should pretty carry
gospel to ugly Garry
only ugly should marry

Robot Love

31)

I have sexually activated my robot ,
unfortunately it has all gone wrong ,
for effect I lubricated her with fish oil
but now she's gone stiff and really does pong
****
Metal fucking bitch , I hope your tits go rusty. :o}

Coping With Change

32)

The changes in time
make me sick ,
because now my clock
goes tock tick

Cross Pollination

33)

Producing much more semen
than I need it has special powers ,
really don't want to waste it so
I start wanking on the flowers .

Thrashing my dick with gusto
putting my testicles through their paces ,
so now my beautiful garden flowers
all have human faces

Life's Rules

34)

Never fuck someone else's wife unless you
really can't remember where yours is ,
don't ever bend down in a communal
shower someone will do you up the wrongun .
Never ever take a bears honey he will
seriously fuck your shit up , be sure not to stone
a stoner for his shit is already fucked up so why
waste a stone. For fuck sake never ask a
cannibal what's for dinner , it's best not to know .
Never get your daughter her own sky remote
unless she lives somewhere else , I'm still suffering
from that one . Always look a gift horse in the mouth
in case the twat is looking to bite you.
Lastly for fuck sake never upset her indoors
during P.M.T   :o}

Out Of It

35)

As I skip through the
valley of death ,
trying to hold on to
my last breath ;
****
I come across the fat
clown of hate ,
carving up human flesh
on a plate .
****
I skip past him , skin
still in tact ,
straight to the devil
to make a pact .
****
Devil's pact in place I'm
then set free .
Wake up in the gutter
full of JD

Trantastic

36)

Sitting in a daydream watching
the ladies happen by ,
when a great big beautiful
tranny got stuck in one eye .

" How are you doing gorgeous ? "
he shouted across to me ,
me to him " get out of my eye man ,
I can barely see . "

Talk about not being able to
see the wood for the trees ,
but from the back he did look rather
good down on his knees :o}

Dogs Life

37)

My mind is trapped
inside a stray dog ,
pricked my nose when
I sniffed a hedgehog .

Never enjoyed licking
the dog's dick ,
then shagging next doors
dog made me sick

38)

Countdown

" So is this a countdown
to an actual event ? "
" Yes a countdown to when
I can spend the night with
Rachel Riley and Susie Dent " :o}

39)

Scarlet Arachnid

Beware the scarlet arachnid
that bitch will fuck your shit up ,
oh sure she will promise you
fantasy and fill your love cup .

Then she will draw you close and
sink her teeth in , back off then smile ;
you meantime will be struggling for
breath , life draining all the while

40)

True Love

My primal screams lure
you to my cave ,
you strut your junk
feeling oh so brave .

Strip each other bare
then misbehave ,
you leave without so
much as a wave :o}

Butt Of The Joke

41)

After her hysterectomy my
wife said strap a dick to me ,
so I obliged her in this farce
then she rode fiercely on my arse ;o}

Private Time

42)

I am not after
anything fancy ,
just spank my monkey
and call me Nancy . :o}

The Best Sex

43)

I've laid with several whores
when I bang one out it's not about her indoors
although I do wear her draws

Horse racing

44)

I took this punt on
a big fat cunt ,
I wish I
hadn't bothered .

One I should have
binned , didn't go
like the wind
he just fucking hovered

Another love poem

45)

Every time her indoors cooks
I get the Tommy tits ,
I don't know what the fuck she
does, she's got no fucking wits .

Burnt fucking this and burnt
fucking that , one time
I'm sure she tried to serve
the fucking cat

46)
Hey fiddle fiddle

Hey fiddle fiddle
the cat done a piddle
the cow came all over the moon
the little dog laughed to see the cow come
and the dish said fuck off to the spoon

47)
Coming out

I'm coming out of the closet
for once and for all
because I can't get any sleep
it's too fucking small

48)
Rain dance

I see you dancing
in a rain storm
clothes all soaking wet .

Your clothes have gone
all transparent ;
I see your nipples pet

49)
Food of love

Music is not
the food of love

it's the pussy below
and the tits above

that are the fucking
food of love

50)
Ogre

I am an ogre
I am 15 feet tall
the kingdom of choice
is mine to fucking call

51
I don't but I do

I don't do sex
but I do make love
I don't argue
but I do resolve
I don't go pooh
but I go to the loo
and there's no semen in me
just funky little boatmen

Fly

52)

A fly sat upon my wall
not knowing what to do ,
so then I crept towards it
and fucked it with my shoe

Cider goggles

53)

I'm sure I saw
a fly eat a spider ,
I really have had
far too much cider

Happy rising

54)

I woke up this morning
as happy as can be
put away my boner
and skipped of for a pee

Happy days to you all. :o} XXXxxxXXX

Printed in Great Britain
by Amazon.co.uk, Ltd.,
Marston Gate.